This is How You Disappear

Jeremy Reed

This is How You Disappear

Elegies

for the Beautiful Very beautiful Agnieczka

ENITHARMON PRESS

Love Jerem

First published in 2007
by Enitharmon Press
26B Caversham Road
London NW5 2DU

www.enitharmon.co.uk

Distributed in the UK by
Central Books
99 Wallis Road
London E9 5LN

Distributed in the USA and Canada
by Dufour Editions Inc.
PO Box 7, Chester Springs
PA 19425, USA

ISBN: 978-1-904634-43-0

Enitharmon Press gratefully acknowledges the financial support of
Arts Council England, London.

British Library Cataloguing-in-Publication Data.
A catalogue record for this book is available
from the British Library.

Designed by Libanus Press
and printed in England by
Antony Rowe Ltd

ACKNOWLEDGEMENTS

Many of these poems first appeared as beautiful, hand-printed booklets, for which the author would like to thank Stephen Stuart-Smith of Enitharmon Press, Richard Livermore of Chanticleer Chapbooks, the Temenos Academy, Peter Baldwin of Delos Press, the late Alan Clodd, Alan Anderson of the Tragara Press and John Robinson of Joe DiMaggio Press.

for Carole Berman with love and deep gratitude

CONTENTS

This is how you disappear
out between midnight

called up
under valleys
of torches
and stars

Scott Walker, 'Rawhide'

'As soon as we have embarked, in order to travel along the arteries
of the subterranean city, upon the dark tide of our blood as if upon
some inner Lethe with its six-fold recesses, tall solemn figures
appear to us, approach and then drift away, leaving us in tears.'

Marcel Proust, *Sodom and Gomorrah*

And the car reverses over
the white cliffs of Dover

John Balance

ELEGY FOR DAVID GASCOYNE

Three streets away from where I write,
plane leaves wallpaper Tanza Road,
their floppy, star-shaped autumn mush
mashed orange round your old front door –
your 1930s sanctuary,
a base from which to walk all night

across the city's meshed network,
its bridges and financial grid
appearing almost visionary:
you hungry, drugged, and looking out
for the dawn's first campari blast
to colour red over Southwark.

Your walks to me are legendary,
deep night as a complicitous state
to constellating metaphor;
the poem memorized as hot,
then worked on by those molecules
which are its individual chemistry.

Bartok and Berg were your thrashed mix
of soundscape geometries, hit hard
into your fine-tuned, shot-down nerves.
You rose at noon, wore pinstripe suits,
a studied tie, saw London burn
in a heat-flashed, war-time apocalypse.

So often, David, I still meet
your benefactor from the time;
her speedwell-blue eyes, blue like yours,
with recollection, while we talk
through leaf-fall, with its mosaic
mottling the toad-spotted wet street.

Today, with sunlight bottled into haze
like colour in an ice-lolly,
I stand on Kite Hill and map out
the city's rudiments – your beat –
a gold star on Canary Wharf
sighting above the compact maze.

My memories of you are late,
your 1980s rediscovery;
we sharing readings, you benign
and anecdotal, telling me Breton
wrote in green ink, Crevel violet,
with total recall at the Tate.

You checked your watch compulsively
for an appointment neither made
nor kept, a secret rendezvous
with time itself, outside de Chirico's
station, framed by a dark green sky
dissolving boundaries of reality?

You gave your life to poetry,
demanding nothing, went insane
like Hölderlin, your gift burnt-out,
and revisioned with dignity
the art of silence, made of it
a sort of abstract creativity.

Poets are born to give and not receive,
the story of our damaged lives
in making out: you sold your books,
your everything, no back up then
as now, just a fraternity
attempting somehow to survive.

Breton you agreed, was the last
to raise a cosh for poetry
as revolutionary credo.
Expelled from the group, you remained,
post-ECT, its survivor,
an undercover surrealist.

Your letters, I have 63,
punctuated reclusive years,
your blanks in time, no impetus
to get back, just your memories
tuned to past highlights, showing like a film
in which you were the commentary.

You are a legend to the few
who know your journey, and I feel
your presence in the smoky air,
the youthful poet, red bussing
to the West End, and Zwemmer's Books,
sometime in 1942?

I write this in a small café
you would have used at South End Green,
aware this poem's our last meeting place,
a point of contact I sustain
no matter unilaterally
throughout much of the foggy day.

You would like me in going back
have climbed the hill by slow degrees
and heard the Thames-link train address
the neighbourhood, and deep in thought
have pondered on the swimming leaves,
the red, the yellow and the black.

LOVER MAN (OH WHERE CAN YOU BE?)

in memory of John Wieners

You died in March, with bitty snow
surfing the viburnum's white spray,
knuckle-shaped sweet japonica
and sarcococca's breezy scent
pointing up spring, and pink cherry
choreographing the window.

Poetry's like a glass half full,
or half empty? Its measure's song.
Your ear was pitched so rhythmically,
you scored notes like a blues singer
working the page with improvised
phrasing like a sweet mama's spell.

Your books are cobbled by my bed,
small press survivors winning out
their time and place, infiltrators
that keep on going, hold their own,
staples and all, the wear and tear
picked up to be read and re-read.

The men you loved, the men you lost,
left you lonely as Jazz FM
heard in the small despairing hours
with rain outside counterpointing
the need to write, and a blue fog
feeling its way in from the coast.

You lived head full of Lady Day's
commiserating, grainy tone,

her small voice as your journeyer,
a habit just like heroin,
her purchase on each song, like yours,
a desperate need to have the moment stay.

A fifth-floor walk-up on Joy Street,
your home for twenty years, no books
to allow room for solitude
and slow-burn memories to keep
a tenancy, live parallel
with your resigned sense of defeat.

Your line mixed Black Mountain with jazz,
crossed East to West, took in two coasts,
part streetwise, part elegiac,
the Beats cocktailed into its graft,
it sashayed across the USA
dressed in feathers for Mardi Gras.

All those asylums, thorazine
and ECT; the delusions
inseparable from poetry;
you broke, head-cased, ruined by
state hospitals, but winning back
to have a sassy lyric shine.

Poets so intensify life,
it seems like film, a walk-on part
in imaginative reality.
We stay there, and perpetuate
extended youth, each metaphor
a ripe peach threatened by the knife.

Impossible to let you go
or ever imitate your style.
You wanted to be Jean Harlow
or Jackie Onassis – the vamps
dressed up to kill, and slinkily
doing it all in slow tempo.

You leave a broken-hearted legacy,
an empty flat, an incomplete
bruised dialogue with poetry.
Death won't give words back; what you gave
is what we have – the line marked up
and staying there unalterably.

You dropped out, circa 1975,
burnt-out mid-journey, broke and ill,
sainted by small-mag alumni.
Mystique sustained you on the hill,
that and a diva's obduracy
in spite of the odds to survive.

You'd known death too often to die
without insightful clarity,
it's something picked up on the way
that deepens simultaneous
with getting there, and then dissolves
like vapour burnt off in the sky.

Today orange tulips crack under rain
scored like car-hoods by big round drops,
stalked anthers gaping from black throats
in Regent's Park. I test your words
the way a bruise colours the skin
as a blue substitute for pain,

and back home, play it to your memory –
Billie's 'Lover Man (Oh Where Can You Be?)' –
the one you never really found,
and hope death's a new start for you,
and listen, as behind the beat,
she makes the sadness sound almost happy.

ELEGY FOR ALAN CLODD

December fog smokes on my hill,
a cold, vaporous secondskin,
a furry chiaroscuro
I punch holes in, out scaring up
a rhythm in its white halo,

your death still loaded in my nerves,
the Royal Free like a monitor
behind me, where a morphine shot
discharged you, screened off on a ward
humming with medical data...

Dear Alan, I reverse the years,
as though friendship clones a shared gene
coded for access in the cells,
and sight you with familiar books,
12,000 stashed against the walls,

stacking the house, a pulped forest
rooting its printed weight indoors,
you massaging a signed *Waste Land*
like stroking silk, Eliot's neat,
diffidently legible hand

frozen in ultramarine tracks...
Your partner George played Bob Marley
a floor below, Jamaican, camp,
solicitous, I see him still
dodging into your desktop lamp

announcing a chicken ragout...
If incongruities design
a menu for purposeful love,

you had it, two making out good,
and in the process fugitive.

He died of AIDS. I'd meet with you,
after your visits to the ward,
his T cells down to 1 or 2,
pneumonia lighting a red exit sign.
We tried, but words wouldn't ring true

in nailing your anxiety,
and stared over tea into space,
you forking a Danish pastry's
raspberry-hubbed cyclopean eye
into a Bacon autopsy...

You came out after George's death
as liberation, wore first jeans
at 70, regenerative,
alive to grief and patterning
a breezier way to survive

by opening inside your loss.
Your bibliophilic mania
provided retreat, each new find
demanding others to complete
an order structured by your mind,

the need always outstripping gain.
You clued your books with pencil marks
and clear diagnostic info
like commenting on a pathology
always advancing through the slow

tropism of paper, boards, glue,
towards inevitable decay.
I see you in the West End grid,
white thistle tuft of stand-up hair,
slow pace editing out the speed

that seems to have the pavement move
with throbbing ante, distracted
by a window in Cecil Court,
your bricky holdall weighted down
with purchases, the handles taut,

you out on your itinerary
via Museum Street to Lamb's Conduit.
Shy man, reserve in you was integral
to a quiet humanity,
your self-invention pivotal

to ways of living true and free.
Your flower was the sweet william,
its bunchy introspective tones
bleeding dark reds and coral pinks
into a slow-tempo maroon,

a subtle palette like your own
deeply textured consistency.
I look for you in every crowd
jostling on the Charing Cross Road
black cabs competing in the loud,

exhilarating, heady rush
of being dead centre to life,
as though the world turned at its core

below that precinct, where the join
at Little Newport Street gains roar,

and yet to the acclimatized
seems oddly quiet – your old patch –
and look up at a sky turned green
this crazy diamond afternoon
in January, and see between

the browsers in a shop window
a book you prized, and live again
our sharing of a gay café,
First Out, underneath Centre Point,
and kick my direction that way

towards its scarlet fascia,
and wonder where and who you are
in the big change, and how you'll be
without your friends; the rush hour now
building around me like an angry sea.

ELEGY FOR KATHLEEN RAINE

High summer. Cool blues, clear contrails,
my journey over seemed unreal,
the King's Road viewed from a red bus
like footage – a girl on one foot
examining a snapped spike heel –

little sightings I made the day
you faded in and out of death
hating the Chelsea Westminster
still word perfectly quoting Blake
as the instruction on your breath –

'To Mercy, Pity, Peace and Love',
undulled by morphine or your heart's
chaotic arrhythmia.
I looped the cord through your white dressing gown,
the act so oddly intimate it hurts

in recollection. Twenty years
a friendship with no argument,
you taught me all reality
is imaginatively conceived,
the poem as the big event

the Big Bang in our neurochemistry.
Whisky at six: Lapsang at four,
you baked me madeleines like Proust's
from a hand-copied recipe,
the orange tincture taking store

of a contesting lemony subtext.
I see you standing by the kitchen door,
wisteria's blue raffish dreadlocks

nosediving into pink camellias,
your scent and clothes from Image d'Or

imparting style to dignity
as an aesthetic: you were first
in taste and in simplicity.
Outsiders were our meeting point,
the mad, the visionary, the lost,

the singularly intransigent,
the ones who lose by giving all
to poetry and win life back
as a posthumous deficit.
Cecil Collins on every wall –

you made your life at Paulton's Square
into a needs autonomy –
your Blake books shelved in an alcove,
your work-desk busy with papers,
a blue clothbound notebook for poetry,

a lived-in expeditious sitting room
patterned by your bright signature,
the individually molecular
data inside a poet's cells
making the space particular

to you, like sunlight trapped inside
a potently recurring dream.
You brought nature to your back door,
the urban jungle outside – the King's Road
fastlaned to a metallic stream

of Range Rovers and Cherokees,
jeeped paramilitary professionals.
Your little precinct shone a light,
brought news of archetypes, was home
to a star jasmine's waterfall

trailing white flowers round the front door.
You called yourself Blake's secretary,
spent thirty years inside his skin
decoding DNA starbelts
of hallucinated imagery,

reclaimed his new Jerusalem
sited in part in Paddington
as the gateway to the cosmos.
Friend to your own, antagonist
to junk layers of academe,

you understood love, every love
as the reverse of death, the light
we give each other that's so transient
it won't hold up, but shared becomes
a star inside burning that bright

we measure it against the loss.
You were the perfect confidante,
unshockable and knew it all
the good and bad, the broken hearts,
and how pain is the quotient

that turns the story into art.
I'd take the river in visiting you –
Cheyne Court, Mick Jagger's 60s

aristo mansion there as a landmark
the river tracking green and blue

liquid film under drizzled light.
Your moment in time, now it's lost,
dissolved into the universe,
the individual burnt to ash
and atomized. What you feared most

was leaving friends behind and speech
the choreographer of our thoughts.
Beauty was your ideal. You closed your eyes
inhaling scent from the held flower
and did that with the peonies I brought

you on your last day, their deep pink
filtered on your breath like a dye.
Blake was Lambeth and you Chelsea –
a London vision mapped across a grid
in which the city was academy

to its shape-shifting instructors.
'All my life I've worked like a black',
you told me, showing no respite
at all in your continuous
single-minded solitary work attack.

Death deepens knowledge of a friend
by recreating incidents
in memory that never die.
Each time I left you was an end,
it felt like that, a small event

matched against the finality.
I write this in the stunning heat,
the summer turned delusional mirage
the notebook shouldered on my knee
and work directly on the street

to feel the city in my veins,
the weight and urgency you knew
around you all day, every day,
as a co-existent heartbeat,
an energy just passing through

like poetry and learn to stay
with what you gave each special friend –
a part of you so individual
it keeps on living – I choose compassion
as your legacy to help mend

damage in all of us, like the poet
committed to heal with each line,
a personal hurt his starting point,
a friend's another, then the big reach out
across the universe to make words shine.

LATE ROSES

in memory of Elizabeth Jennings

Death's clean, if we live true to it,
insighting messengers along the way –
the jackal-faced archetypes or the pointers-up
confirming that we're not alone
in reading signs that get us there.
You braved it all for poetry,
lost out, went under and went mad
amongst the disassembled on a ward
and learnt how small things save, a peachy rose,
the calm space found in a Utrillo on the wall.
The Mind Has Mountains niches on my shelf –
your 1967 best,
a book I trusted in my first breakdown
for its amazing lyric clarity,
its quiet thrust in turning round the mind's
disordered undersides, and finding there
regenerative poetry.
You lived with a conviction that few dare,
one life, one art, the unity
strengthening the trust we're cared for when we care
so little for security.
You wrote in cafés, wore blue lumpy coats,
the poems always coming easily.
October was your terminal time out:
death's a one way, with no reporting back,
even for a poet obsessed with giving shape
to lateral encounters. Autumn gold
hangs in on these pink roses tucked
by the back door, their life-extension plans
keeping a late appointment with the sun.
They're mine, they're yours inside this elegy

we share, and would have made a gift for you,
three candy-coloured roses holding on
before they die to a perfection won.

ELEGY FOR ALFRED MARNAU

Lo Spuntino, 1983,
our King's Road meeting, sky-filled eyes
talking blue Adriatic space
into the room, big-screen blue skies
windowing as their metaphor
poetry running like a road

out of the heart across Europe
the way your blue Mercedes chased
a long burn-out trajectory,
you in pursuit of a lost place
to still call home, a retrieval
from visionary topology…

First meetings, and they never end
in their updated legacy,
you citified me with your taste,
your cultural rightness, poetry
our building block like DNA
to reading life, an energy

that sped along your arteries.
Our mutual passions: Rilke, Trakl,
death-bound, Octoberish poets,
their celebratory elegies
turning on loss, and Hopkins too
with apple-round vowels on the tongue

brought spotty autumn to the room.
Your Eyre Court days, all books, heirlooms,
sanctuaried in NW8,
Kokoschka on the walls, the night
increasing outside, always night
inside the poem like a date

with an elusive stranger seen
and lost again as soon as won.
You bit so hard on living, death
prospected sweetness by contrast,
you lit each moment, caught the ash
and telescoped nine lives in one.

Your beauty was the living proof
of your aesthetic, head-turning
feature-refinement, Hollywood
missed out on your heartbreaker looks,
the slightly quizzed affirmative
undying image of romantic youth...

Autumn again. You've missed this one,
its rainy early-dark presentiments
chasing up red leaves on your grave,
compact, familiar Highgate plot,
you knew as yours. Bruise-coloured clouds
obscure a laid-back hazy sun.

Where do the dead go? Webster's lines,
was the conundrum you would probe,
caught by a red light in Mayfair...
Now you've the answer, I the pull
of the unresolved quandary,
remembering the shock of hair

that kept the child alive in you
begging blue-eyed simplicity
as one way in and out of life.

Always your generosity
upgraded life for those you loved,
you of so many kindnesses

the increase dazzles in my heart.
Your absence is a star gone out
receding from the galaxy.
Three dark red Bokhara roses
were what I left you at the end,
you who in dying learnt the art

of letting go your passionate
decree to live at any cost,
closed the last door, prepared to trust
love as your guide, as though a friend
had come for you to light a way –
the one road to the great beyond.

PALACE GATE

in memory of Martyn Sinnott

The Bentley wasn't yours; you nicked a wing
zigzagging on the flyover, burnt West
from the main concourse, 'look no hands' –
your risky up-there dynamic when coked
imparting crazy flash to how you drove

to win the precedent at every light.
Your clubby years, no focused energies,
sensation always pitched to overkill,
then lost again, you ran up every stair
to punch the rainbow in the chandelier

and come down disillusioned by the dawn.
You torched your youth and never wanted more
than to derealise before the crash...
I see you dragged-up in outrageous mink,
bitchily witty with camp repartee,

disarming friends, but always in reserve
compassionate, as though a kindness won
the deep place in your heart. Our zippy days
return now shocking pink azaleas
overcrowd with their hectic ballroom gowns

in every London park, dramatic reds
ready to sashay the season's catwalk,
then tumble, turned over by raunchy winds.
Sometimes I lift the telephone to hear
it ringing in your old palatial flat,

as though by a freaky coincidence
you'll intercept the call and say 'I'm back,

death offered no more fulfilment than life.'
Your jumbled, heirloomed rooms at Palace Gate
spread out their contents in my memory

as though I'm back there, you so shot with AIDS,
the virus worked you cell by losing cell,
the undercover clever breaking down
your every resistance but dignity:
you lying wrecked on a pill-hailstormed bed.

We'll never know each other twice the same.
I work in time with all the busyness
you envied once, and you are open space
as I conceive it, someone, everyone,
a reincarnation with a new name?

Our big nocturnal happenings, the trust
we placed in love and death: now you've known both
and ripped the red curtain protecting youth
from rapid exposure, and hurried through,
impatient you said, to begin again.

Drug cocktails extended your legacy.
You lived for whiskey and sweet memories,
before they too were wiped. I buy you flowers
today, to keep you near: a heady shock
of rain-scented, abundantly clear-eyed

and piercing jonquils, and see you again,
this time in full health running for the car
with expectation life lay round the bend,
the clear road open wide beneath the stars
and in its curved reach pointing without end.

YESTERDAY WHEN I WAS YOUNG

in memory of Dusty Springfield

Mimosas, dear, forcing lemony scent
into a cold reactionary March wind,
I bought them on the day you died
to raise a yellow torch in memory
of how your voice addressed our needs
in every shade of love that's blue
and shared with us its aching entreaty
to find a little sunshine after rain,
a sanctuary from bruises dealt
invisibly across the soul.
Today, your death-day, you are on the air
posthumously, your husky R&B
slow-burners building in their rise and fall
smokily pitched delivery.
Your life returns with every anguished catch
in phrasing, you the bouffant blonde,
the patron saint of mascara

wreathed in a boa, lending signature
to how the song hinged on a frantic sob
to make the pain definitive…
I keep on hearing retros of your voice
as though you're still singing familiar hits
six hours after your death. Big purple clouds
arrive, dispensing hints of flashy showers.
You've gone away, like someone takes the train
with no-one knowing, no address,
no destination, no reporting back
about pure music on the other side.
We listen to you in Freedom, First Out,

and hold you near this way and celebrate
a torchy diva's dramas, feel the hurt
in your vocal authority,
and hope you're healed in passing, wish you where
the light in its entirety shines through.

Sainthood: Elegies for Derek Jarman

SAINTHOOD

The river swallows thunder; cold gold nerves
sheathed in its spinal undertow:
it keeps on filming clouds stoned by the light.

Someone's in trouble diagnosed
penitent HIV. Their viral load
reads like a print-out from the galaxy.

Sainthood's conferred by heavy rain,
it's like the red rose swallowed by Genet,
found in a ruined cemetery.

What's it about a man converting earth
salted by sea-winds into flower
speaks of the street-crowned apotheosis,

the jeaned Soho iconoclast
transforming everything he saw
to lyric as it opens in a flower?

Life's a reminder that we die.
The gutter takes a footprint and returns
the indentation of pure gold.

A man cries out at Charing Cross,
his moment used up, but continuous
in what imagination colours blue.

He's here to stay. The autumn surf
gobbles a shingled gradient, ejects
slow-release burials in its shattered tow.

PEOPLE COME AND GO

She'll tell you in her phrasing, love and death
meet at the apple's core; the yellow skin
bruising sweet black. The words travel her breath

as torchy consonants, her sequins drip
like red flame sheathing tropical fish.
She coathangers a right hand to her hip.

When he remembers the black diva's tone,
he dips into a buzzy memory.
An apple cuts its bootlace, thuds on stone.

Memory's like a clouded lily pond,
Elizabeth and John Dee look up through carp.
There's Pasolini windowed in a bond

with broken things. The sea turns frisky jade.
He feels the T-shirt wring wet at his ribs.
The viral heatwave allows for no shade.

The dead are transparent. They're light on light,
programmed into their separate energies.
Big purple thunder clouds surf through the night.

The living never outnumber the dead.
The diva's melody springs back to mind:
it's Gloomy Sunday; he retrieves the thread

and hears the sea leave white shoes on the beach.
He lives inside the moment. It is round
and almost orange and just out of reach.

BURNING BRIGHTLY

Summer means poppies: splashy opiates
tangoing with a swishy breeze,

giving the big come-on in fuming silks,
rubbing their dusty eyes with black,
dresses in scarlet tatters, frizzy stems

notched with green Adam's apples, or the white
and purple opium poppies sleep
in a vision of the dead

sleepwalking in a slow cortège
arms lifted heliocentrically to the sun.

Somebody waits there in the noon,
a man in contemplation of his life
as though he stood in a mausoleum
hearing his voice go pleading for

a little respite from the cold
that's underworlded in his blood.
The sea sounds like it's slaughtering a bull
across the shingle. Feedback roars

through a haze spooking the coast.
He stands in discourse with himself,
head bowed, and hectic poppies prove

consolatory, burning bright
and fragile, like a lip trembling with love.

LOVE IN DEATH

All day, the traffic's ambient decibels
surf around Phoenix House, its flat façade
presenting on the street. A white noise shell,

the building's atomized by toxic haze,
its windows click-tracked by the diesel mash
of black cabs streaming up to Centre Point...

Somebody's absent from the honeycomb
and uncontactable. He's gone away,
leaving a trail of sand down Brewer Street,

as though he'd walked in beach shoes to his death,
thinking the sea was on the other side,
a blue invasion of Piccadilly.

The inspirational genus locus gone
from his packed studio, we have the word
resituate his fireballed energies

in every meeting place where we collect
to burn a torch beside the river's groove,
or wait for love to hurry through the rain...

Say that we recreate the little things
that gave an apple-polish to his life,
a coffee-tang to being just a man

alert and vulnerable to everything,
then he's still here, beating in every heart,
catching the raindrops and making them sing.

UNDER PADDINGTON

Rain over Paddington, and underground
chimeras ledge on obsidian thrones.
They'll drag him into death through corridors

serviced by no communicating line.
A messenger in a red coat will lead
his impulsed holograph into the maze,

somebody newly arrived from a day
busy with doctors and invasive drugs,
a man nerve-sheathed inside a hologram,

still formulating scenes he'll never shoot,
or paint, the reverse mirror-side of light.
He'll see his guardian's feet have dark blue soles.

The Circle line is coffin-shaped. The map
he reads, as he imagined it, is blue,
the youths who give him flowers know he's dead.

The garden's somewhere, but it's not his own,
wired up with driftwood totems, blasted by
the wave's white thunder fuzzing on the air.

He can't turn round on the committed road;
his name is typed into the microfiche.
The boys around him spray his aura gold.

London's behind him. There, it rains all day.
The river's foetus carries a new god
shock-waved along its lightning-twitchy spine.

RETRIEVING ANGEL

Whose is the hand extended in the dark?
He doesn't see the face, the concave back
shimmers with vertebral translucency.

The psychopomp's uplifted feet are bruised
with pink magnolia petals. In the park
the youths transmit after-death frequencies.

His flashback-recall is to Hampstead Heath
with outlaws grouped beneath an orgy tree,
the rainy oaks brimming with violent scent.

He's in a garden, and it's mauve and blue,
the urns are packed with rubies, glowering jewels.
He has to check himself for *déjà vu*.

The one in front has shoulder-length blond hair
and answers in awareness that's so fast
that thinking has become pure energy.

Two red-haired angels dressed in leather jeans,
are watching new souls on a monitor.
The dazed arrivals twitch at memory,

then quickly relocate to being there.
He presses on; the light is clearer now.
The angel looks round. He is in his teens.

They keep on moving. It's like going home
to meet himself again in the deep end
of a wild garden's blue compacted shade.

SITES

A warehouse burns in solid orange flame,
erupts at Bankside, a black cumulus
of tented smoke pyramiding the Thames.

He sits and contemplates biography,
a Persian carpet rages in the sky,
voluted purples peacocked into green,

a fuming skylight over Canon Street.
A city's dawn is always visionary,
he strokes atomized stardust on his skin,

as though chasing gold embers from his pores.
His studio is torched. Two years go by
memoried under bridges, blued with tears,

the same trains hustling into Charing Cross,
the changes registered inside his blood.
A day is like a pick-up which won't stay

faithful to anyone, despite the need
to have it open out into a friend.
Bugloss and borage present to his eyes...

He paces memory like it's a room
in which the furniture comes clear at dawn,
a blue vase loaded with redundant dreams,

a red one choked with flowers, he clears the lot
to know the moment, catch his breath again,
and feel the city fit him like a boot.

OBSEQUIES

Sits in a gold sequinned gown on the shore,
a man blasted by toxic chemicals,
increasing, as his T-cell count
zeroes like stars receding in deep space.

Is it the sea's stony dialectic
at Dungeness, invites his charged
inventiveness to know itself
bright as the dazzle blow-waved off the beach?

Or listen along the South Bank side,
where time sits on the river's back,
a blond boy in a beret drops
a dented beer can in the tide,

as a small death in memory,
washed away in the cloud-piled afternoon,
like youth gone downstream to return
decades later as someone else

burnt at the edges from a different shore.
Yellow horned poppy tugs its roots,
resilient like scabious.
The hand that planted is tubed by a drip.

An anchor's ochre rust erodes
a staying power that won't go,
an object obsoleted by the sea.
With man it's different: he can't get back

to know himself again, not twice the same.
This one's ending is Derek's, cell by cell,
as though the sea forced inland, wiped the lot,
but left a camera pointed at the clouds.

ELEGY FOR KATRIN CARTLIDGE

Pre-dark October, 4 p.m.
aqua sky detonating pink,
you broke out of the Hampstead woods,
an oak-tunnel's stunning leaf-fall
of violent appetizing reds

clashy with up-tempo orange.
We fitted in each other's heads
almost colliding under spray,
you'd read my book, the instant rush
of spontaneous telepathy

mixing our words, like two colours
transformed that instant to a third.
Spacy, tranced-out, interiorized,
you still in character, and I
tuned to a poem's frequency,

met through a sixth-sense nerve-radar,
immediate, while a panicked bird
signalled its territorial claim.
We shared a street at South Hill Park
coincidentally, but knew

each other from an inner space
dissolving all reality.
Our meetings, always at the one café
were like journeys across a map
taking colour imaginatively,

configurative inner states
we claimed as our own territory.

Our afternoons. Your skin leaf-wet
from walking, fog still in your hair,
the season fleshed into our speech

like taste-buds popped on the palate.
We thought each other here to stay,
even that last time by the car;
your profile in turning away
detaching, so I keep it still,

an image burnt into my brain,
eyes downturned, sensitivity
so filigree it hurt, the rain
beginning as a film-noir theme,
its slow staccato continuity.

MISSING

for Rolf Vasellari

The Regent's Palace, twice a year,
your Piccadilly in-transit
hotel, you in from Zurich's clear
lacustrine air, black biker boots,
black leather jacket, eyeliner,

emaciated as Artaud
at Rodez, your mad role-model
for the pantheon of outsiders
from Jean Genet to Kurt Cobain
you adopted as prototypes

for a punkish social disdain.
You'd meet me Hampstead Heath bus park –
Swiss chocolates in your shoulder bag,
books, CDs, gifts you'd found for me
with an obsessive's need to share

an underworld mythology.
Lithium for dysphoria,
your manic cycle peaked and dropped
like a free-falling base jumper,
you jerky and once in the street

hallucinating desert tanks
exploding into sheeting flame.
We'd walk the foggy East Heath Road
up past Boy George's gothic stack,
oaks dripping in October bleed

and plateau at Jack Straw's Castle
and drink there, you cuffy Guinness
and me an ordinary red.
You'd feed me writings, surreal plasma
raw as a Pollock, visceral

as hara-kiri, and drink hard
to rapid cycle the effects.
Outside, the early mushy dark
grew grainy. A last cerise slash
of sky sunk over the carpark.

I'd recreate your work. Our bond
was spiking literature with rogue
hallucinogens. Risk the lot,
was our belief, lose everything
for running with the underworld.

You disappeared without a trace,
joined Richey Edwards, Weldon Kees,
and all the permanent missing,
your body gone over a ridge
or sucked into the river's muddy lees?

Today, the white fog at my throat,
I track a sticky gradient
uphill, towards our familiar landmark,
my head full of you, an acute
revisioning of little things

attached to loss, downing my mood;
and see you as you were, skinny,
afraid, and on a jumpy fuse,
matching my fast pace through a fuzz
cold as a jewel, and live again

the highlights of our last meeting,
your upbeat tempo, born to lose
was what you said – and the phrase stuck –
you running for the bus that night
unable to turn round and wave.

FOR INGE HOY RASMUSSEN

October. Brash, termite-scored orange leaves
littered Lyndhurst Gardens' sedate
Belsize Park precinct. Eden Hall,
you dying in my neighbourhood,
the houses stepped out of Magritte –

white mansions glowing in the dark,
you far from home and foggy deer
scratching their antlers on the bark
of your custodian oak, its thrust
forcing up out of centuries

of leafy photosynthesis
to throw its arms over the house.
Your brightness shone in everything
like the blue diamonds, green opals,
the ice-storms you prized in a ring's

eruptive, scintillating blaze,
your dealer's acquisitive eye
matching the stone for clarity.
You lived antiques. Your aesthetic
translated into a bijou

Art Nouveau furnished Copenhagen shop,
you choreographing London finds
like a miniature Northern Lights.
My visit. Holte 2000.
We sat out nights beside the lake's

lapidary, obsidian eye,
the big oak as an umbrella
and watched fireworks calligraphize the sky,

your daughter Lene's platinum hair
so blonde it seemed a waterfall

frisked through the trees to join us there.
We spoke of Kierkegaard, his mad
compulsions, and the naval yard
he walked around, tooling his thoughts
to metaphysical plasma,

and of your husband's black Topolino,
the car he reassembled, part by part,
obsessively reconstructing
its dynamic, his oil-streaked face
showing up indoors, like a pits

mechanic, greasy from Le Mans.
We looked up and a rocket corolla
nosedived in pink stars to the lake.
A fox broke cover. Its radar
sending it back into dense trees

shivering with leafy reprise.
Your death was long-haul. Then quiet.
The morphine tracking through your cells,
the street outside so oddly like your own
it comforted, you fading out

on such a white surrounding light
it seemed to pick your thinness up
and carry you off like a deer,
nervous at first, then finding out
the forest path shone bright and clear.

GUNN DEAD

The Teddy boy, all rebel cool
circa 1956
in skinny jeans and biker boots,
insolent, tough, the image mean,
the attitude like Jimmy Dean
posed by a street lamp in leather.
The poems mapped the metaphysical
constraints of finding in the real
a car-buffed resolution won
with the tricky scoping of a Wyatt
or a leftfield John Donne.
Later, you came out and the poems fed
on San Francisco hip and drugs
done for recreational chill,
bath houses and rock festivals,
men that were like your paradigm,
masculine, but soft the way
a resilient sensitivity
typifies gay.
Your work increased, casual, humane,
finding in loss, the Aids die-off
a recombinant theme:
death and the outlaw, viral loads
tracking through cells like SAS.
A late compassion: it was tried
against a generation's
suicide.
We miss you with your line as clean
as veins in a nasturtium's leaf,
neat, economic and symmetrical.
You died, a youthful 70,
alone in bed, life-force still optimal,
your work unfinished, it's the way
to leave the parts unequal to the sum.

OUTSIDE FOYLES

in memory of Adam Johnson

The Foyles fascia. Orange O
coronal as a tomato,
I saw you there once destabilized,

HIV facial atrophy
tagging you with a cratered dermal map,
your poem 'The Departure Lounge'

still hotly garaged in my memory.
A big city near miss: we shouldered by
with the trancy autonomy

of two depersonalised by the fazed crowd.
I could have turned you round, called out your name,
but left you in the rush hour corridor

tunnelling to the underpass.
Ivory raincoat, blond hair louchely raked,
the retro-virus tracking through your cells,

you went underground at Tottenham Court Road.
Today, out surfing on the West End rush,
I have your posthumous book for review,

a slim-line *Collected Poems*,
a catwalk Size 8, a cucumber waist,
the poems fired-up with hot imagery

jabbing glucose into my brain.
The book's your epidermis now,
Adam reduced to cheap paper and glue,

but palpable, unlike you at the end,
a rope trick with a helium lift.
Another rush hour: the volume full-on,

I check into its racy overload,
your poems as companions, the Foyles sign
there as you knew it, real time Martian red.

ELEGY FOR JOHN BALANCE

Soho in whiteout January:
we stood on the corner of Brewer Street
fired up by spontaneity, the shock
of cold forgotten, and the place
lit by your signature that day,
the sky a blue diamond, an 80 carat rock

brutal, up-front, indifferent.
Something of you came through to stay,
a look retrieved by Fresh and Wild
I keep in me as permanent,
you as you were without your pain,
the little pearl left by a child

untarnished in you to be found
and polished by a happy mood.
You who were reinventing Coil
lifting its dark chthonian energies
out of mystique into live act,
doing a Bartok to industrial

edginess, lived to be that band
with Peter, shape-shifting the sound
in ways so individual
you were its origins, the deep
keepers of a textual palette
coloured by death, but beautiful.

I'd seen that look another time
at Oak Bank, with us kept indoors
by fog smoking in from the sea
stacking its white fins in the bay,
a solid opalescent wall
we couldn't see through, shimmery,

that had you glad to be inside,
filling in blind spots in friendship
things that we'd never shared or knew
about each other that came up
bringing hidden reserves to light
to be spontaneously added to.

You fought depression, scary stuff,
like lights out in the underground,
cracking drug foils, or using drink
to drown the monster in its own fluids.
But that week you held back, deterred
from forcing limits to the brink

by friendship, and the warmth we kept
maintaining in each other light.
Today I recollect your eyes
that searched a painting vertically
extracting detail from the whole,
looked upwards, quizzical, surprised

in that slow, quiet way you did best;
and how when we last spoke you talked
inventive seasonal recipes
for mushrooms come up like blotchy UFOs,
lentils and squash, a soup you cooked
rich as Shakespearean tragedy…

You inscribed CDs in silver
hieroglyphics done with a marker pen,
a mapping that was circular,
loopy, intuitive and fresh
as a newly washed salad leaf:
on one a snake swallows a shooting star.

It seems your guardian went missing the day
you crashed over the banisters
backwards to end up on your head,
the trickster prone to accidents
still muzzy from a reckless binge
impacting and instantly dead

at 42. I walk the heath
under brilliant cold sunshine,
your green shirt on my back, a Nigel Hall
gifted from you, a scarab green XL
roomy on me like a jacket
three sizes too big for my Small

and feel grief shift around in me
without a shape or diagram,
just violent mood swings, up and down
like turbulence rocking a plane
and kick through blood-orange red leaves
drifted above the gold and brown,

aimlessly walking Highgate way,
still talking to you as a friend
about the journey I can't share,
the one you're on, the frequencies
time lagged like galactic e-mail,
but sense somehow you're getting there

by a light distinctly your own,
the blaze that shone in you those times
you channelled inspiration into song

and shaped it to your need aware
of its potential as a gift
so pure it had no right or wrong

but chose you for identity.
Your open coffin as an end –
we faced it in the lowlight Woodlands mist
writing last messages on paper squares
for you to take like confetti
into the fire, and stood there lost

as you were carried off alone
in a black carriage led by a black horse
along a puddled drive to disappear
at the third bend – a stand of trees
commanding view and winter clouds
big on us, like they'd never clear.

ALAN (I NEVER KNEW YOUR OTHER NAME)

Even at 30, silver hair,
a Rolls Royce colour inflecting the black.
You kept a Hockney book on the counter

at Victor's Mens open on *The Splash*,
that blinding aqua blue theming
a new come out mythology.

I saved for months for a cashmere crew neck,
a schoolboy rebuffed by the price
who window-shopped French labels

on empty Sunday mornings.
The hurt you carried turned in me
like a knife an apple

rooting amongst its heart-shaped seeds.
Summer seemed permanent like pop
and blond a signal of iconic youth.

I met you once at La Colette
and saw again the loneliness
you carried like a foggy day,

linked it to death instinctually,
my mother's, and to a stripped down same-sex
excruciating vulnerability.

Victor's is now a Sushi bar
and you programmed into old age
are still a 40 something memory.

Back home to see my mother, I look out
for you in every street and fear
changes in you I can't meet in myself

or her – the hurry to the end
that picks up speed and once seemed far away
as a directionless, blown-over cloud.

SU

Your black tumbling curls
like grapes on the vine
in the right light you're twenty
not multiplied by three
looking like Sandie Shaw
at her leggy
apogee
in your black clothes and leopardskin
thin as a pin.
You sit with your grief
on an orange velvet cushion,
your lover dead, his grand piano
a Bechstein sarcophagus
an ebony elephant
with discoloured ivories
like yellowing snow.
We're two under the skylight
by a blue twinkly lamp
that leaves half the room
like the dark side of the moon.
You play me Tony's last blues
done in a leathery overcooked voice
a week before his death
as a valedictory wail
a muddying of roots.
He built this floor and jungled it with plants
fleshy Tropicana
pink gingers and yucca.
Your poise is so balletic
it's like yoga:
you're like a black winter pansy

perfectly weighted on its stem,
even your grief in balance
it has its deep place now
in you the flower untouched by frost,
resistant to the snow.

WALKING IN THE RAIN

for Biddy Crozier

Violets tugging microphone leads
flex in the April London rain,
their hounds' ears petals folded back

like words prompted to poetry.
You came into my life, the gift
of a closed uncommunal neighbourhood

circa 1987, blue eyes
full on like Blake's with wacky analogue,
searching me like a tracker beam

outside a café, the September sky
the brash green of an unripe lemon.
Friend to the oddly-themed, the dispossessed,

we met by synchronicity,
as though we'd planned the moment, set it up
by broadband telepathy

to have it fizz like a poured Coke.
You'd sheltered David Gascoyne, given roof
to his vagrant poetic banditry.

He threw knives at you as the finale
to discontinued patronage.
Egyptian earrings, a patterned sarong,

a stick for one arthritic hip,
you were my pavement guru, quoting Blake
for back up, like a supplement

vitaminizing subtle energies.
Your look was deep as double bass.
You wore age like a shimmering aura.

89 years. The tiny violet glowers
in stringy rain, dull scent shut down
as though dissolved into the steady pour.

ELEGY FOR MICHAEL ARMSTRONG

Your heavy Pringle cable-stitch –
off white, oatmeal or navy blue
perennial comforters, crew neck
and lived-in were your signature,
bought at De Gruchy's, an XL

loose on your acorn-shaped body…
You were my mentor at 19,
the friend assigned me in rehab
from burn out, breakdown, mixed-up youth
doing its self-destructive thing,

heading for a 737 crash.
I'd phoned Samaritans in pouring rain,
crammed down too many tablets on the beach –
two-tone nose cones of Librium
and waited. Your bashed Volkswagen

stood in the car park. You walked out
towards me and we met like that
incongruously, drenched and beat
a quick retreat into your car,
the coast a blinding, fuzzy blur

of blue murk over the harbour.
You published my first book *Target*,
my scrunched youthful precocity
packaging compressed imagery
into redundant firepower,

the little book an incentive
to keep on living? I made tracks
to London; and our friendship grew
by letter, like the pink camellias
you coaxed into exhaustive flower

each January, their tough green leaves
glossy as car upholstery.
I'd come back home. You'd bake a cake
big as the Ritz: the brandy popped
from cherries in volatile hits,

you opting for a second piece,
a cautious third? Your library
pushed weights on an entire floor.
You painted abstracts. Loud colour
steamy and hot as Africa.

You loved life more than anyone
I've known, your kindness giving back
your easy independent means.
Your window on the bay dissolved
into a slash of blue and greens –

a shimmering vanishing point...
You seemed too permanent to die,
too earthed, too habitually part
of living, spooning rum baba
under a white beach umbrella,

three books open to read as one.
You dying, I wrote letters every day,
remapped the points where our lives meshed
significantly, saw you walk
into an unlit corridor

inside my dream – you'd lost your way
but were still you right to the end,
and woke and knew you'd disappeared
into the tunnel and gone on
distracted, as though looking for your car?

JACK'S

out of my past. You dead on me;
I'm safer now to close sight you
this Soho day, as imagery –
nitrogen dioxide air quality
40ppb – forecast low:
the right ecoclimate for elegy
that I've deferred? – I write this way,
direct inside the city's mix,
my DNA mapping its corridors

my brain messages fast on Bateman Street –
you in my neural highway (Jack)
Jack's elegy put back ten years,
fear of his disapproval blocking it,
as though the dead were a pathology…
I take a through across the grid,
St Anne's Court, the graffiti tag –
death really sucks like Jimmy Dean
involved in recombinant energies

boosting the poem's samples – you and me
those years ago, furred by the Suffolk night,
your village like a space station
lighting up the surrounding dark,
a bottle on the table, Auden's books
firing up NY anecdotes:
he'd blown you in a loft on Bleecker Street
and me your confidant – I hear
your breathless forty-a-day monologue

infiltrate as I cross the street,
buy Mojo in a newsagent,
a bar of Lindt chocolate 80% cocoa,

dodge an off-roadster, rehabilitate
your voice to scrambled memories,
lose it up front, sighting a jeans logo –
a neat, embossed 2X4 leather patch
I detail in before retrieving you
outside 20th Century Fox

in Soho Square – the poem still on air
reluctantly, and again put on hold
as a flash-forward possibility
the light around me swimming green and gold
like hallucinatory autumns we shared
out on your lawn, only the city lacks
tonal deepenings, red frogskin leaves,
and me the incentive to write it down
this elegy that's almost Jack's.

MAX

A wasp in a stripy T-shirt
kept gunning the oozy ring-pull can,
buzzy with hypoglycaemia
its reverb inside tin walls
like a fidgety helicopter.

Summer was stringy egg-white clouds,
you naked, sunning on a ledge,
the sea turned lapis lazuli.
I the inquisitive spectator
confused you with my father,

Max who my mother turned down
sensing gay undertones
to a diffident proposal,
became in my mythology
a surrogate protector...

All August, sunstruck, surfy glare,
the coast a menu of found things
retrieved by a deep coma tide:
starfish and bottles, gritty shells
lidlessly rattled in the wash.

I watched you and backed into shade,
my head stoned by the full on sun,
saw you pick up a bleached blond youth
and returned to the shore afraid,
confused, and stung by jealousy.

You were the suity lawyer
done for indecent exposure,
who scandalized the locals
by flagrant same-sex bravado
tangoing by the harbour

within sight of a Shell docker...
You drove a dark blue Jaguar
around the coast, defied the law,
and lived under a black halo
disqualified from chambers.

You dead, I reverse building blocks,
reorder time – the night we spoke
blue thunder clouds massed skyscrapers
above the bay – we tilted back
beneath an overhang, shared space

from the explosive trashing storm.
Your shirt was a crushed strawberry
blotched on your skin. Hair mashed by rain.
Electrons charged the crackly air.
You broke at the first interval

leaving me compact in the dark.
I scratched your name into the wall
weeks later, and today persist
in substituting a fiction
for truth, and claim you as the one

who individualised my chemistry.
You died in March, the snowdrop's hood
turned to the earth, and never knew
the bond I felt, snow patterning
from sea clouds rolling into view.

ELEGY FOR BERNARD STONE

Shyly garrulous, 5' 3" or 4,
backroomed inside the shop, the hangovers
loud as the Heathrow corridor
deferred by 10 a.m. vodkas, scarlet
as a full-on winter sunset –
the bottle crisp from the office freezer
blued over with condensation
like a full length silver fox fur…
Drink (95% proof)
kept you above the bottom line
you never showed; the solitary
who partied but went home alone
and faced the bathroom mirror agonized
as a Francis Bacon.
Your generosity was effusive
and had poetry fizz alive
at Turret. You were its mover
by force of personality, the quiet
philanthropist, twinkly, casual,
your repartee like play fighting; the twist
never acidic, but dissolved
in laughter like a mixer.
Expert deferential philanderer,
reckless hedonist, you became
a patron saint to poetry
in your 1950s dark blue blazer
and slippery tie, star attraction
at readings, your conversation radar
crunchy with gossip, spiked with fun.
Upstairs was the arena, wine-stained books
blotchy as though rained on by mulberries,
downstairs the proprietorial lair

and tissue-wrapped first editions cellar.
Your kindness shone in everything,
maverick, bon vivant, a cigarette
caught in a hand dropped to the hip
like a gunslinger. You made names
by stepping back, your louchely film noir style,
old world, attentive, finger to the lip
in confidence, wet oil-licked hair
done like a thinning Dirk Bogarde,
your dependants were others' successes,
your personal life off-limits, buried deep
inside the music that you made
humming your way to work through Russell Square.

LARRY

6'4", black American,
you were the bonus to my only job
as empathetic secretary
to Jonathan: (I'd seen the ad
in *Gay News* – Denis Lemon's seminal
Kensington coterie editorial,
a fizziness in being gay,
not queer in 1981 –
a broad pink stripe slashed across the city).
You answered the front door, head up
in a galactic chandelier,
a coruscating chunk of blue and green
Northern Lights: white shirt and white jeans,
and snaked upstairs like a morning glory
opening momentously into the light.
Jonathan wore a white slouch hat indoors,
employed me instantly on looks,
(you'd disappeared to make the Fortnum's tea,
an Orange Pekoe): Larry the houseboy
at Pembroke Gardens, deferentially
compassionate, immersed in books –
Nocturnes for the King of Naples,
your favourite chocolate box of metaphors.
Jonathan's tempers blew holes in his blood
like a machine gun fired from the brain stem.
You rode the turbulence, then ran away,
a giant escaped back to Washington,
the shock waves impacted like an earthquake
in Kensington – the house shut up and dead
for weeks: no flowers, no cake making,
no shirts pressed like a central marker-line,
no laughter rising like a head of beer.
Today, twenty years later, we still write,

trafficking memories: Jonathan dead
or missing, like the smudge of wiped brain cells?
You worried for him, like we still care now
in ways he would have cherished, build on this
as our sustaining theme, we let him down
or didn't? you a college librarian,
and me still writing poetry, make sense
of loss and gain, like cherry blossom blown
in little red-eyed bits all over town.

ASA BENVENISTE

The thin one. Belsen, Dachau-thin,
black T-shirt under a silver
cashmere V neck:
your voice smoked from Camel filters,
a quiet New York inflected baritone
resonant as Leonard Cohen's

phrasing from a thoracic well,
each word selected for its body weight
in gravity.
You wore a Saturn-shaped blue opal ring
like a poem, sparkly planet
drawing the eye to its slow-burn pulsar,

my first impressions circa 1970,
a foghorn blowing growling sax offshore,
you flying in and out that day –
here for my burn-up poetry
you claimed had a leopard's heartbeat
inside its detonative imagery,

a flavour, just like Rimbaud, so you said,
in hallucinated intensity.
You wanted twenty-five for a first book
from Trigram; you the handsetter
raising ink off the page like a cobra,
its bite into paper so clean,

you felt the raise like black nail gloss
as the printer's signature.
You were London's small press cult publisher,
bringing me books – Raworth, Jim Dine,
injecting trust in me to have my hand
walk like a shoeless nomad on the line

I still keep now. You ate yoghurt
instead of meals, and got race circuit highs
from volatile Turkish coffee,
published outsiders with impunity,
worked at your own poems, a Jewish rite
of fetching kabala to verbal chemistry,

and had the tree of life tattooed
in black and scarlet on your nape.
You got me to London. I owe you all
the shape-shifting miles I've tracked on the page.
You died an amputee, your left leg stumped
like Rimbaud's, eaten by diabetes

and gangrene.
Your chess partner was a whisky bottle
progressively losing out its level
to your tried hangover immunity.
Your last poems were like morning glories,
lyrical, blue, scented like the Tangier

you'd lived in 1953.
I see you still, the foggy day we met,
me naïve, disingenuous, and you
already my instructor, thin blue jaw,
saying half in humour, but more in truth,
poets only live by breaking the law.

MOO'S ELEGY

Little orange streetwise stripy,
oracular avatar,
one of Haringey's homeless
fetched home in a basket,
your purr was a nasal motor,
a rumbling of the vocal chords
like pre-prepared piano
or accelerating thunder.
You were the tricky jewel thief,
a tabby kleptomaniac,
making raids on Lene's mother,
retrieving rings upstairs
and absconding with their glitter,
as though your teeth were capped
with diamonds and green opals.
A pampered domestic slacker,
your radar tuned into poems
read out on rainy autumn nights,
you buzzing demonstratively,
red in your fur like a tiger,
the garden coloured like squash.
Irrepressible, bouncy hedonist,
undeterred even by diabetes,
you warmed to the needle's jab
in your neck's compliant cushion:
and strutted your rhinestone collars
a diva transformed at night
into an urban guerrilla,
mousing the way an owl trails
the tail like a skinny bootlace.
Your fur had the smell of weather,

each season lively in your coat.
You brought the moon indoors, and slept with it
as your instructor. You were attitude
and treated as an equal. Now we pick
a qualifying rose to badge your urn,
and count your collars like a pharaoh's funeral stash,
half imagining their sparkle
compounded into your grey compact ash.

SOHO JOHNNY

Wisteria boas a trajectory –
blue tassels lipping lilac tusks
outside my basement, NW3.
May back again, another year
underwritten like a scar,

you missing and your viral load
at last contact optimal,
HIV and drug-induced psychoses
wiping your system, you offline,
anonymous as the concourse

at Piccadilly Circus underground.
Your poems feed me gritty craft –
two books from a co-operative,
signposting youth and manic obsession –
your cloning fix on a singer

whose bed you shared on Brewer Street.
Tantrums and karaoke scenes,
he threw knives at you in between
diva spectaculars
recording 'Vermin in Ermine'.

You're like a quantum particle
existing simultaneously
in two places – dead or alive
body-bagged in a mortuary,
or living, blasted by your cells?

Your letters scored in orange ink
read like a Burroughs narrative,
a drugs lab pharmacology.
Your poems, two or three winners
don't come better and stick with me

in what I remember when out
city-busy and giving space
to deep probe issues, they come up
as comforters, familiar lines
like street names mapping out a place.

GLENISE

The heiress to a Berger heir,
red hair
tied back, a bullet-nosed cigar
dipped in Sambuka for flavour,
you stood, hands on your hips, intransigent,
your life ruined at 25
by his obsessively perverse demands –
the man who didn't want to die
and sat up all night linked to consciousness
like a pilot radar,
his mother mummified in the next room,
rocks on her fingers raying out
like cool blue scintillating stars.
You had to change her jewellery once a year,
as though the dead gave precedence
to possessions and noted luxury
from a post-human body.
He broke your esteem systematically,
wished you would age contemporaneously,
accelerate like a BMW
tailing to overtake his years
as freak biology –
Glenise flash-forwarded to 82?
Your Havana flared with a red nostril.
He called you Sister Death, the butch
attendant on his end.
I'd stand with you out on the balcony,
the sea always the colour of the sky,
the coastal villas shelved like light boxes
into the hills, and think deep, deeper still
for you and how you took it, gave my thought
a blue consistent with the bay,

a gravity tempered by trivial
observations conceding to laughter,
at how he spoke for three hours on the phone
some nights to my mother, and neither remembered
a word the other said, but shared a space,
a point in time, each valuing
the contact to feel less alone.

GERARD

Part Berber, part Andalusian,
part Mill Hill East,
the gene cocktail showed in profile
(the nose a little angular):
the eyes a winning point, their hurt
dissolved in avocado green:
Gerard slumming it at Pembroke Gardens,
commandeering the red master bedroom
in return for lurid, virtuoso repartee;
bare torso and chunky gold chain,
giving his rap to castanet
hand movements in the mirror.
Dressed in black skins, uncreased leather,
he worked the best hotels as rent,
the Park Lane Hilton and the Dorchester,
an infiltrator to each floor,
a fugitive with attitude,
knocking at random on odd numbered doors –
a favourite 1, 13 and 33,
his tactics mixing outrage with the shock
of uncensored availability,
room service in return for wads
of notes thick as a dictionary.
He brought the dirty money home
and scooped it in a crystal bowl,
dissociating from serial numbers
he'd sold out for, and stayed fascinated
by money as an exhibit,
as though it was a snake in a vivarium,
dormant there, sleeping off its kill,
an energy he feared to touch
for retribution, a python whose scales
were crisp red £50 notes, mauve £20s,

autumnal browns. He'd tell us to dip in
and liquidate the poison. Gerard dead?
I got news from a friend, who'd worked his patch,
shot through with Aids, one of the dispossessed,
pre-anti-retrovirals, scorched by plague,
and recollect him doing a karaoke
'Love For Sale', one hand on his head,
the hurt in him pleading what have I done
to myself? the bay window behind him red
with a hazy late afternoon on dimmers Earls Court sun.

RANDALA

Our last time, fuming orange poppy red,
the late sun over Pembridge Road,
Notting Hill Gate, the solar core
sighting us like a traffic light,
you in a fake leopardskin coat

blotchy as pebbles on a beach,
wrecked by your mother's meltdown death,
the cancer tracking through her cells
like traffic on the motorway,
virulent rogue agents switched on,

accelerating without remission.
We sat in Starbucks talking Venice Beach –
your wooden shack facing Pacific surf
and tumbled clouds at the world's edge
and took in the faux-Murano

pendulum lamps, my green Zen tea
steaming like a rainy summer meadow.
Twenty years back I saw you read
your poems unforgettably,
words lifted out of analogue

into digitised imagery,
your black hair bunchy like wisteria,
your voice smoky with vibrato,
your black skirt fitted like a flower stem
in a pub room above Queensway…

Our friendship first at St John's Wood
then coloured all over London
like rampant garden nasturtium
tugging at orange umbrellas,
lived in me like a fine-tuned mantra.

You biked across the NW grid
to meet me in cafés, a psychonaut
carrying little gifts like cake
and honey. Your voice rounded words
like water mapping a pebble.

Apart now, I recall the day,
a blue cloudless July mirage
we met on Hampstead Heath and claimed
the shelter of a giant twisted oak
and for an hour knew time stand still

and right brain fears like age and death
dissolve in shimmer, let it go
the drive to live and sat trancy,
speechless and staring at the light
and for the moment absolutely free.

MARY ABSALOM

The tidal drop was 40ft,
the shore like a postcard from Mars
sent across 105 million miles,
you mixing a mule-kicking martini
for a space programme in our cells,
red Oreal hair, black YSL dress,

ubiquitous black, your trademark
invariable signature.
You were my surrogate mother,
a feisty diva turned psychic,
a medium to big shots, the Guinnesses,
corporate hoi polloi with flaws,

speculative venture capitalists.
Your first floor was my sanctuary,
a window open on the bay,
the sea a murky aquamarine,
we sitting listening to Lou Reed
narrating X-files on a Factory queen,

the night arriving, inkjet black,
a star-shot slab over the coastal towers.
We were each other's stimulus
for my post-grad vacations home,
my head full of John Ashbery
and leftfield New York Francophiles

disrupting lyric rationale…
Your birthmark fascinated. Upper lip
twisted with a rhomboidal splash;
our anorexic phenotype –
you 6 stone and me barely 9
of hyperactive energies,

had us share clothes for nocturnal
forays into the Side Door bar,
its underground gay milieu
exploding across the dance floor,
a strobe light tracking silver walls
with a pink holographic star...

Your loss was Johnny. The rent boy
you'd shared a flat with in Queensway,
a platinum meat-rack raconteur
who filled you in on every scene
from nude cleaning with a feather duster
to pick-ups underneath the street.

You gave me taxi grants, brokered
my belief in extravagance,
and are my role model today
for living in the moment, fast,
immediate, juicing the page
like the hard shoulder of the motorway...

You sold the house and moved away,
relocated to the city,
the two of us dispersed across
the metal jungle's anonymity,
you East, me North, the divide felt
as abstract, unquantifiable loss.

We lost each other through the years,
hurried down windy corridors
that open on the universe.
Age, you would say, is like a helium balloon
defying gravity?
My mind keeps coming back to you,

the story incomplete, you gone,
but backlit in my memory,
head slightly thrown, small mouth exclamatory
with life's surprises, the harbour backdrop
framed in the window, the violent sunset
like hara kiri drenching a white shirt.

BERT

Extravagant three sea-blue variants
in each hydrangea's cupola;
your stammer overdubbed the consonants
with jerky vibrato,
got stuck second syllable 'a',
then let the misnamed genus go.
You drove a grey Morris Minor
colour of sea-cloud dragging by,
parked it above the docks, maintained
fugitives live by afternoon,
soft-focus men need empty time
was your advice, time out
from regulated systems,
the luxury of being free
to fill the self, stand back on granite stairs
tricking descent to a harbour...
Our 3-4 p.m. sea-meets,
me in a green cashmere jumper
you claimed matchmade a stop-by hour,
you with a flattened Penguin squashed
boxily into a jacket;
me 16, you 72,
laying a groove so deep in me
it tracks there still, resilient
subtext to living on an edge
and dangerously.
You fed wild cats, loved Tchaikovsky
and men in dinky angora,
read my first poems, rooted out
their adjectival overload,
and laboured speech the way the sea
scrunched pebbles as raw phrasing.

You died on me, but reappear
each time the afternoon grows taut
with expectation and high cloud
smokes over lazily;
me with my slow-hand liberty
to write the day through remember
your maxims and our last goodbye,
blue hydrangeas bushing our walk
bittily blue as washed-out sky.

ANNA PORCELL

A winter redhead, summer blonde,
Anna Porcell's like poetry
the obsession I can't get to
no matter how familiar.
We see each other, like a film –

our own take on *Last Days in Marienbad*,
her stylised gestures creating
a choreographed aura to mystique.
Her perfume's Creed, indelible
as porous registration plates

coded into tanned Latin skin.
She's hot like poppies in the sun
and keeps a Lorca poem
hand copied in a roomy leather bag
that always smells of autumn.

We met ten years back in a bar
beneath the Everyman, after *Orphée*?
Now older, damaged, we're alert
to emotional saboteurs
and vulnerable don't risk the hurt

that comes from spontaneity.
We keep our own side of the street –
her wave is like telepathy,
a signal we attract, a buzz
inside a neuron like a bee.

Anna's the change I write around,
the seasonal journeyer, the one
who moves in and out of my writing view
outside a neighbourhood café,
black V-neck jumper, sprayed on jeans.

Autumn again. The day stands still,
the light's coloured like lemon peel.
The summer's programmed in my cells.
Anna appears as though on call
at 3 p.m. – I watch her go

towards the park, as though my life
disappears through that avenue
of blotched plane trees, recedes with her
by edits, while the leaves freckle
under a sky that's spacey blue.

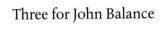Three for John Balance

FIRST OUT CAFÉ

Our meeting place. The lower floor's
subterranean sanctuary,
grey fascia, 52 St Giles High Street,
you pouring vodka in a liner-shaped
defiant wedge of chocolate cake,
the orange tincture particular

to your approval. You'd surfaced
from weeks of catastrophic drink,
a compulsive inspired debacle
landing you up in A&E,
your liver the size of a dinner plate.
I read you lines from the Upanishads

about dying through the top of the head
as a sort of ejector seat
ensuring the right pathway out
into the sun. You brought me books,
Poems of Death, Freak Meteorology,
and spoke of living for 500 years

like a deep-rooted forest oak,
the acorns raining from your beard.
Our café built on a plague pit
seemed appropriate now a strain
had re-emerged as HIV,
another raid on immune deficit

restocking London's mortuaries.
You worried that you couldn't sing,
the impetus used up at source,
a circuit closed inside the brain.
I spoke to you in metaphors
of a stream sliding round a stone

unobstructed by the impediment.
Your dreams were like elephant's bones
dug up after centuries of decay,
the jungle in their calcium.
Your shoulder bag rattled with supplements
and feel good chemicals like valium.

Each time we met was like the compressed space
a poem or song occupies
in impacted intensity:
the meaningful on its measured bandwidth.
We'd climb back upstairs to the London day,
a pink light dusting St Giles in the Field,

and hesitate a moment on the street,
as though care for each other's safety grew
proportionate to vulnerability,
and was always our last thought, the big fear
we kept inside, turning to wave and watch
the other pick up pace and disappear.

TOBACCO PLANTS

Their roots are sixteenth-century, Marlowe stuff,
transported from Virginia,
sweet scented flowers, your gift to me
in a nursery seed packet
wedged between hand-painted CD covers,
a gold and purple psychedelic swirl,

or star-belts shaped like blue Viagra pills
proliferating across galaxies,
the mappings of a shaman colouring
his access to the visionary.
Some days I think I see you in the street,
vigilant where its spinal curve

accedes to a scarlet mailbox,
lopsided, dislodged, like it's drunk,
and panic at the thought you're dead
but still around in my reality –
sloganed T-shirt, sea grey jacket,
eyes submerged in their commentary

on thought shapes swimming into view.
Back home, your flowers are shoulder high,
leaves the size of elephant's ears,
tubular flowers all pointed down
like an inverted plate of spaghetti,
narcotic postings on the breeze

attracting my nostrils like a bee.
I sit with the essential earthiness
rudimentary to you in everything
you did in your green world, appraising stems
much as I imagined your spine
was leafy between vertebrae

and terminated in oak spray.
These are my meditation point,
my union with you, and a slash
of red nasturtiums do undercover
between their spread, and a late sun
is coloured like them an explosive Etna red.

The summer deepens. If the dead move on,
then you're in process, while tobacco flowers
are for the moment my immediacy.
I trap the sun, and their effusive scent
invades my patch, as though my sitting out
has made a small into a big event

in which you feature, you who bonded green,
and stood with me once, each on our own side
of a great oak, and felt its healing rush
accelerate through the rough scaly bark,
our fingers joined, and like today the sun
optimal red an hour before dark.

POND LIFE

September light's like champagne poured
all day, an atomized dazzle
of Moët & Chandon.
I sit out in it decoding a dream
in which you swam with Chinese carp,
only like them you had red fins
and a black and white marbled jaw
and disappeared through a tunnel
into accelerating dark.
I watch the subterranean Fleet River
begin its journey underground,
its muscle pumped out from a Hampstead pond
that shivers like compliant silk
at each new annotating breeze.
I hear the river's introductory pour
before it goes under as soup
fed through the city's arteries,
black water infected with dioxins
and London's shattered immunology.
The light I sit in shines like orange peel
on leaf and aquatic detail,
and seems in its arrival from dead stars
a cocktail of indifferent energies
turned for a moment on my hand.
Somebody fishes in the urban flow,
defiant, waiting for a murky bite
to scatter the float's equipoise….
And you, the fish-bodied man in my dream,
swimming so strongly in your red-scaled skin,
will you return tonight, cruising your way
into my deep-sleep underworld,

your ripple electrifying my spine,
and point to the direction that you took
last night, the way the lazy Fleet goes down
pulling with it a carpet of sunshine?

PAULA STRATTON

I come to meet you twenty years too late,
Temazipam spilled all over the bed
like a pearl necklace shattered on its string
at Chester Gardens, you already dead,
your red curls stabbing the white sheet,
your books and things, The Glass Bead Game,
scattered around you, and your goblin ring

now turned dispassionately cold.
You died at 28, your overdose
a last defiant act of liberty,
the lonely, drug-crammed exit that you chose
irreversibly final as the door
locked on a Boeing at take off.
You'd left a jigsaw puzzle on the floor

of Tolkien's Journey through the Middle Earth,
the pieces scattered as component bits
of your fragmented, incomplete journey.
The man you loved, your dealer, was the pits,
blue sunglassed speed-freak Dave, banged up inside
for selling rafts of dodgy LSD.
You couldn't break his strangulating hold

on your emotions, or the drugs he fed
your confused, chaotic dependency.
I used to stay with you at Strawberry Hill,
lie in your attic mapping poetry
and synchronize our love of small detail
by looking at an oak leaf or snowflake
until we'd transformed the thing totally

by trading likenesses, a visual game
best qualified in autumn, when the street
swam with the violent clutter of silk leaf.
You had no place in life, each new retreat
a friend's room, or a space found on the floor
invested with your aura, like the sun
had risen indoors. Once I heard your name

called out behind us at Piccadilly,
and it was Dave, and you were gone again
to his white powders and mean underworld,
his dirty money dampened by the rain.
You were so pure, and he the opposite,
but couldn't help yourself. You clung for life
to what he gave you, raw, injected pain.

You the idealist, never had a job,
but waitressed periodically, and were
insider to a vision you explored
as your reality, a journeyer
who lyricized a dream. I see you still
in a red velvet coat in Richmond Park
dancing between the trees, arms open wide

like their forked branches overhauling breeze.
Your letters reached me in their naïve hand,
round as an apple, written in transit
chasing a festival for a hot band…
They'd arrive as effusive fat packets
twinkly with drawings, you'd seen the Pink Floyd
playing so high they seemed to stand in trees…

The breakdown came before you faced the end.
Dave hurt you so hard he was like a wall
you ran against, each rejection harder
until the pain itself wasn't the fall,
but how to live with it and still want more.
Your disappearances grew more prolonged
as though you'd stepped into a corridor

with all the lights out in the underground.
You had it planned of course and took a place
in which to die, and personalised the room
and chose your moment, leaving not a trace
of negativity in words you wrote
your mother and young sister, raying out
your orange sunny feelings in a note

that never once conceded to despair
and trusted in the pills as a clean end
and kept the light on as a comforter
as though it was a last indifferent friend
against the final dark, and died that way
not knowing where to go or who you'd be
beyond the ordinary London day?

JANINE

You read Anna Kavan as panacea,
legs arched in a pink Biba micro-skirt,
one liquorice black knee boot slung over
the other asymmetrically,
the sun lounge windowed on a bean green sea,
an offshore tower like a granite chess piece
apparent in the fuzzy coastal haze.
Your look was quintessential 70s,
your mania archetypal, down then up,
the low resistant as a flat grey stone
washed by the sea. You played Leonard Cohen
obsessively,
Song Of and Live Songs 1973,
his voice frozen like cracked Russian rail track,
25 minus zero baritone,
like scooping out a snowman's heart.
Your up was an excitable self-harm,
a calligraphy written on your wrists
with razor blades, a Basquiat
you mapped out autonomously.
They fried you with electric shock
burning your spiky, nervy poetry.
You fell in love with Anna Kavan's pathology,
her syntax clean as the white heroin
she gunned into her veins.
Her books were an aberrant gene, you 22,
and sitting on a polar cap,
that solitary. At low tide reefs cropped up
like Mars rocks, each a chestnut mare
streaming with manes of yellowish seaweed.
We walked the shore, a scrunchy ecosphere
of dropped in meteors, rocks from the sky.
Your eyes were chocolate diamonds:

your family hung up on madness as social taboo.
We sat and stared in amethyst rock pools,
teasing a rayed out sea anemone.
Time seemed to stand still. Twenty years later,
adjusted, medicated, you left me
a voice message on the day that you drowned:
you'd sent me a painting – *Beach at Low Tide*,
a purple abstract scrolled into a tube
as a gift post-dating your suicide.

An 82-year-old Marlon Brando,
your hair dyed beach blond, sandy gold,
effusive to the velvet coat collar,
you drove a fire-red Alfa Romeo
convertible, a scorching shape-shifter
burning the bendy coastal road

as though you were still 23,
not broken, stringy as an Afghan hound
circling its own tail like the tree
it's chosen as a place to die.
You lived on bananas and insulin
and Cooper's smoky Lapsang Souchong tea,

mismanaging your diabetes
with KitKats, chocoholic sugar hits,
and going off-map searching for a vein
to stick the needle in. You never slept,
afraid that if you did you'd die,
and sat up all night, staring out to sea

wrapped in a blanket, a lighthouse
signalling like a white slow-burn quasar.
You stashed your properties with junked antiques,
the pile up like a looter's hoard
of scrambled treasure gutted from bank vaults,
a four million pounds legacy

dispersed by Christies at your death...
You had your mother mummified
in a glass box – it scared me cold –
the incest you confessed, her being there,
her bandaged body wrapped in white and gold,
the house lights on all night, the bare

bulbs throbbing like conical eggs,
opalescent planets stalling the dark.
Your pet crow, Topsy, gobbled cheese,
legging it on your shoulder, broken wing
spread like a shattered umbrella,
feathers black as a funeral car.

You were the guardian of hurt animals,
but not yourself, a Great Dane, twenty cats,
a barrel-bodied Labrador
called Nimbus, with a black halo,
that used to lick the convalescent crow
hopping to gain advantage on the floor.

Your eccentric misanthropy,
I swallowed it like a drug at 20,
and saw in you the perverse saint
flaming in my aberrant cells?
I was the witness to pathologies
burning you out, the crazed delusional

obsessions flaring up at 2 a.m.
that you'd been poisoned, off the wall
paranoia that you were really two,
your double waiting for you in the hall?
Death seemed so close, it smelled like car leather
upholstering your biffed vintage Daimler...

Your voice, I have it on total recall,
the tentative stammer, the fractional
delay in connecting two thoughts
as though a gap in the circuit
had forced apart the carriage and the train:
a voice so quiet it had me concentrate

on each inflection and retain
the sentence like an undulating fish
still browsing fins up in my memory.
You'd made friends with the German Commandant
in the occupation, 1940,
and sold him antiques, your duplicity

rewarded with good wines, the swan
you dined on in burgundy sauce
while the populace grew endemic thin.
Years later, you had a house torched
by arsonists, who left a gutted shell,
and tagged your car with Nazi graffiti –

Heil Berger for the Iron Cross…
Your live-in assistant was 23,
Glenise who loved you like a rope
bunched into convoluted knots.
You, the starved elephant were impotent,
your yellow tusks dropped on the ground,

your mind working to substitute
a tricky metaphysic for your loss
of libidinal frequency.
I watched resentment twist your life
like hara-kiri done with slow
positionings of a blunt knife,

the pain prolonged as mental agony…
It was the dark you feared, black 4 p.m.
in December, crushed strawberry light
swallowed into a purple slab,
your fear building around the night
as regenerative insomnia,

the brain too fired-up on alert
to ever shut its streaming imagery.
No pills worked on your chemistry,
no consolation reached you then
in your exhausted state of anomie,
as though your body was a common hurt,

each place occupied like your mind
with pain that never conceded to sleep.
I wrote all your admissions down
for a defunct, interrupted memoir,
a book pulled from the underworld,
the monster holding up its bloody paws,

the struggle incomplete and desperate.
Glenise lit fat cigars and fumed
at your irascible demands –
your phobic descent into starvation,
a banana a day, or late-night chips
picked at from Sizzles, too soggy, too fat

to coax a ruined appetite.
You wore a desert-coloured cardigan,
a Great Lake in a diamond ring,
and called your house sparrow Catullus
and had the little poet sing
eventfully inside in an open cage

at Tivoli, the house you named
after your mother's habitual resort,
the walls washed fluently by marine light.
I wondered at your impetus,
your resistance to death, the short
catch of breath sometimes at your heart

and just how deep your secrets were contained
like a great oak's defiant roots
acquainted with a site 500 years.
Glenise slept in the bath for lack of space,
contorted, wrapped in a fur coat
beside her discarded black suede knee boots…

I drank or piled in the roomy Daimler
for late night policing of your properties,
a bottled window, no alarms,
an avalanche of books crashed in the hall,
you knew each place as mental geography,
a contents mapping, clear, precisional,

the only light in town a pharmacy's
mint green lettering jumpy in the rain.
I heard your loneliness above
your quiet – you absorbed the night
like pigment colouring your memories
as black on black. We spoke of heroin

as a terminal palliative
or anything that killed a nerve
connecting to a German officer,
your mother, death, your loss of potency,
and tried to find a dealer by the port,
our car conspicuous as an embassy's,

the rain endgaming atmospherics on the roof.
You wanted youth, I wanted age,
you wanted life, I wanted death,
the tragic contradictions so acute
it brought us together; the docks gone dead,
the darkness pushing at us palpably,

your life brought to this final edge
of wanting coffee more than anything
for human comfort in the cold.
You spoke of your mother's gold wedding ring
worn on your little finger. A ship's horn
toted a lonely resonating wail

like jump-starting consciousness from a dream.
That signal seemed a link towards your end,
as though you'd been called out to sea.
Autumn turned smudgy in orange valleys.
You wouldn't eat, burnt thin like fog
as your dispersing energies

turned to inconsequential things
as a distraction. Drips and tubes
maintained a chemical efficacy
reorganizing you, so you could die
less frightened now the morphine overtook
anxiety. We had you try

composure as the state in which to drift
away, but you resisted giving in
to loss of personal identity
and pulled back from the edge each time
like someone troubled by air pocketing
who holds the armrest for support

over a violent squally Atlantic.
Two days, displaced inside a nursing home,
your descent went into free fall,
no bottoming out, you were bone,
the rattle in your throat a castanet,
the dying hard and tangibly brutal,

you drowning on your own fluids
as though a knee flattened your chest
before the frantic breathing stopped
like a car alarm menacing the street.
You'd gone at last to the interior
as a place where all converging roads meet

without direction. In the final heat
they burnt you with your mother to clean ash
liquidating dodgy genealogy.
We waited outside in the fogged valley,
the oaks gummed by grainy November murk,
the raw damp chasing us into a pub

to pick at words that didn't fit
your person, and outside two rainy crows
stripped a ham sandwich, wrestling the fat,
and we quietly turned over memories
like cloud patterns we'd taken for granted
breaking up now and trailing out to sea.